THE RESTAURANT JOURNAL

Waterlane
e d i t i o n s

Vancouver/Toronto

Edited by Elaine Jones.
Cover and interior design by Susan Greenshields.
Cover photograph by First Light.

Printed and bound in Canada by Friesens, Altona, Manitoba.

Canadian Cataloguing in Publication Data

Murrills, Angela
   The restaurant journal

   ISBN 1-55110-953-0

   1. Restaurants—Handbooks, manuals, etc. 2. Wine and wine making—
Handbooks, manuals, etc. I. Moore, John, 1950- II. Title.
TX945.M87 1999   647.95   C99-910847-6

The publisher acknowledges the support of the Canada Council for the
Arts and the Cultural Services Branch of the Government of British Columbia
for our publishing program. We acknowledge the financial support of the
Government of Canada through the Book Industry Development Program for
our publishing activities.

TABLE OF CONTENTS

table of contents

INTRODUCTION

introduction

HOW TO EAT LIKE A RESTAURANT CRITIC

by Angela Murrills

Whether it's the finest French cuisine or spicy Singapore noodles, I'm passionate about what goes on my plate, and writing about it gives me an excuse to eat out most nights of the week. While some critics do get special attention (especially if they announce who they are), most of us don't. We're ordinary folks and we get the same food and service as everyone else. But one advantage we do have is that we know how to get the best dining experience possible.

Trying a Place for the First Time

Let's see, there's that rustic Italian restaurant just down the block that you still haven't been to, and a French bistro you've heard about, and you've seen ads all over town for a ritzy new steakhouse . . . how on earth do you choose where to go? Make the wrong decision, and you'll wish you'd stayed home. Make the right one, and it could be the start of a long-term relationship. It's a lot like a blind date.

Don't just pick a name from the Yellow Pages. Up your odds of success by doing your homework first. If your colleague at work says that Café Carmen serves the best paella ever, make a note of it. Ask your butcher where he goes to eat really good steak. And read local restaurant critics, of course – but carefully. Warning lights should go on if every review is a rave. It could mean they're not picking up the bill, and that "review" is basically an advertisement. Watch for clues that give the game away – "Pouring us yet another generous cognac, Madame du Camembert told us the secret of her poulet sans culottes." You get the idea.

Once you've found a critic whose judgment you trust, try out a few places that he or she recommends, order the dishes they talk about, and see if you agree.

A Little Planning Always Pays Off
So, you're off to that hot new restaurant everyone's raving about. Exciting, isn't it – in fact, why not make a reservation for late Saturday night when the joint will really be jumping? Bad idea. Go when chefs aren't at the end of their work week. Many take Sundays and Mondays as their "weekend." On Tuesday they're fresh, and raring to go.

Worried that your night out is going to melt down your credit card? Call the restaurant, and ask them to fax you the menu or tell you about a few dishes. "And the price?" you ask ever so casually. That way, you'll know what you're in for.

Once you've decided that Chez Jacques is the place, make a reservation so you won't be left cooling your heels for an hour in the bar or, worse, told with regret that the restaurant is totally booked. Even food critics book ahead (using a fake name, of course) and if they can't show up on the night for whatever reason, they cancel, which is what you should do too.

May I Show You to Your Seat?
Never mind how tender the veal was, or how sublime the dessert, if the welcome isn't warm and genuine and the service isn't flawless, you're not getting all that you're paying for.

how to eat like a restaurant critic

Good servers shouldn't tell you their life story, or even their name — unless you ask. Ideally, you shouldn't even notice their presence. If empty plates seem to disappear into thin air and glasses magically refill themselves, that's as it should be.

Listen carefully if your server tells you about the day's specials. These are the dishes that chefs dream up to show off whatever's freshest and in season — and here's where they like to experiment with new ideas. Now's the time to ask any questions. Just how spicy are those Hubba-Hubba Hot Ribs? What kind of seafood is in the casserole? Competent staff will know right away.

What's on the Menu?
Perhaps you had a massive lunch and can't handle an entire three courses. If you just want appetizers, ask for them. If you want to eat three desserts, that's okay too. You're the boss. And if the chef's special six-course tasting menu looks appealing except that you're allergic to shrimp or mushrooms, ask if you can have something else instead. "No substitutions"? Not these days.

It's okay to share, although some places have a small charge for the extra time and care it takes to prepare two separate plates. It's also fine to ask for a spare plate if you want to give your partner a taste of what you're eating. Desserts are so large that requesting one Triple Threat Chocolate Bombe and two, three or more forks won't even raise an eyebrow.

One final tip. If it's a really special evening—an anniversary, say,

how to eat like a restaurant critic

or your best friend's birthday—and you'd rather not spend time mulling over the menu and wine list, call the restaurant ahead of time, say how much you want to spend, and ask if they'll put together a dinner that's within your budget. Most will.

How Does It Look? How Does It Taste?
Did your tastebuds start to wave excitedly the moment that vegetable terrine was put in front of you? Excellent. That's the way it should be. The appearance of a dish says a lot about the care that a chef puts into his or her work. Be wary of overly fancy presentation. A tottering tower of precisely cut vegetables, or too many blobs of different-colored oils and vinegars may mean that more thought has gone into building the dish than cooking it. Whether it's a lemony sauce with a fillet of salmon, or wild mushrooms playing up the dark richness of a well-aged steak, everything on the plate should be there for a reason.

Next, touch your plate. It should be the same temperature that the food is meant to be. (It goes without saying that hot foods should be hot, and cold foods cold; if they're not, send them back.)

Now comes the fun part. Take your first bite, and listen to what your mouth is telling you. Is the dish balanced in terms of flavor and texture? Are the lamb chops butter-tender? Do the green beans still have crunch? Is the sauce silken and bursting with flavor? If you're wondering if that's thyme or tarragon in the *jus,* or where the *foie gras* comes from, or how long the chef simmers the boeuf bourguignon, go ahead and ask. Servers may have these facts at their fingertips. If not, they should volunteer to ask in the kitchen.

Venturing into Ethnic Dining
It's not just Chinese food any more, it's Cantonese or Szechuan or Hong Kong style. Then there's Japanese, Malaysian and Vietnamese, Indian, African and Lebanese, and all the European cuisines: Spanish, Italian—make that Tuscan and northern Italian—Greek, German, Portuguese, and all the different variations of French cuisine. Being presented with a menu in another language can be daunting, especially when you'd like to try a dish that's a little different. What do you do?

You ask. Ask the servers what's in #233 on the menu. Ask the family at the next table who look as though they know what they're doing. If that dish being carried out from the kitchen looks or smells totally delicious, ask what it is.

It takes a little courage but saying, "I don't know much about your food but I'd like to try something new . . ." and then giving your server a free hand is a sensible route to take. Just define the parameters. Say if you're passionate about clams, or can't stand green vegetables, or have a phobia about foods that are white and wobbly. And if you have a close friend who's Chinese, Greek or any other nationality, count yourself lucky. Take them out for a meal and let them educate you about the foods of their homeland.

how to eat like a restaurant critic

how to eat like a restaurant critic

Brickbats and Bouquets

The steak could stand in for shoe soles, and the fish has more bones than a museum. Most restaurants prefer that you tell them what's wrong right away so they can try to remedy the situation. If, on the other hand, the meal has been truly magnificent—one that will live in your memory for years to come—don't keep it to yourself. Share it with those who made it happen. A phone call is nice. A note is something to pin up on the staff notice board. And if you're a restaurant critic, all you need do is write a glowing review.

ORDERING WINE AT A RESTAURANT

by John Moore

For many years, those who consumed wine with their meals in restaurants invariably ordered it by the bottle. Notions of what constituted dining out were derived from a European, particularly French, tradition of haute cuisine and the appreciation of fine vintages selected from extensive cellars. Imitation of this narrow version of the experience, which completely ignored the real, vibrant European habit of frequent, casual restaurant dining, not to mention that of other cultures such as Chinese, often became parody.

We've all had the experience of eating at a restaurant with delusions of Tour d'Argent or Maxim's grandeur which exist only in the minds of its arrogant maître d' and obsequious waiter, since nothing in the ambiance or on the plate can sustain them. Such experiences can be as funny as a Monty Python restaurant skit, except for the enormous bill whose arrival coincides with the onset of indigestion. We have all had to endure a well-intentioned server's reverent "presentation" of a cork painstakingly extracted from an outrageously marked-up bottle of cheap porch-climber (an object we are expected to fondle and scrutinize as if we were reading omens in a chicken liver) and the earnest patience with which a dram is poured and our verdict on the seriously swirled and sniffed sample is awaited.

Unless you're paying upwards of $100 for an older vintage, this is pure pantomime, but it's part of the ritual dining-out experience as our culture defines it. Greeks and Italians lunching in a taverna or trattoria would howl with derisive laughter at such antics. They drink

ordering wine at a restaurant

the "house" wine young, drawn straight from the barrel into carafes or stoneware jugs and quaffed from tumblers, not stem glasses. We, meanwhile, are confronted by wine lists longer than some modern novels. Restaurants not only compete for awards based on the size and selectivity of their cellars, they also pride themselves on the range of their offerings of wines by the glass. If you took the time to read and consider these encyclopedic listings in detail, your stomach would assume your throat had been cut.

Dining out is a social occasion above all. Ignoring your companion and/or guests while you ponderously consult a wine list the size of a phone directory or cross-examine a wine steward is both pretentious and rude. You have two basic options; order wine by the bottle or by the glass. The following tips may make the process less of an ordeal and more of a pleasure.

Wines by the Bottle
As long as public tastes and restaurant menus conformed to the conservative, mock-European model, it was a reasonably simple matter to choose a bottle of wine that would complement everyone's food choices. Traditional wine and food pairings aren't arbitrary; they evolved over centuries for good reasons. Red meat, game, strong cheeses and spicy tomato-based sauces overwhelm most white wines. They need the tannic dryness of oak-matured red wines to stand up to their richness and intense flavors. The more delicate tastes and textures of fish, white meats and soft cheeses would be

obliterated by a potent red. The herbal notes and light crisp fruit acidity of white wines enhance their subtler flavors.

There are equally traditional exceptions, of course. White retsina is the only wine to drink with grilled lamb spiced the Greek way – the pine resin which makes it smell like a glass of floor cleaner is an astringent that cleanses the palate of the slightly greasy aftertaste of the meat and picks up the motif of the lemon marinade and equally resinous rosemary so beloved of Mediterranean cooks. Similarly, rare true pink champagne, the lower-tariff blanc de noirs – style bubblies, rosés, the still blush wines derived from second pressings of Zinfandel or Grenache, even a Beaujolais-style Gamay or lighter Merlot are oft-neglected but superb complements for stronger flavored fish and shellfish: wild salmon, lobster or poached oysters.

One of my favorite restaurant meals used to be a rack of lamb, marinated in Indonesian peanut sauce and accompanied by red cabbage flavored with sambal, the blistering pepper sauce of Java. The best wine for this unusual dish turned out to be a fairly heavily oaked Chardonnay from California or a good Chardonnay Bourgogne. The tannic oakiness countered the richness of the meat, while the assertive fruit mellowed the attack of the volatile spices. A supple, elegant Bordeaux or boutique California Cabernet would have been turned into an expensive but tasteless table decoration by this meal.

This particular dish foreshadowed a situation which currently prevails in many North American restaurants. Menus are so varied and eclectic, so cross-influenced by world cuisines and

ordering wine at a restaurant

super-charged by today's creatively competitive young chefs, that choosing a wine, even multiple wines, to accompany a meal can be a daunting prospect, especially if there are more than two in your party. Restaurants specializing in "fusion" cuisines often make use of unusual spices and flavor combinations derived from cultures in which wine is uncommon or even forbidden.

White wines, especially Rieslings and Gewürztraminers, are the best bet, since their residual natural sugars cool the jets of most spices, but Pinot Grigios (Pinot Gris) and Pinot Blancs, Sylvaners and Müller-Thurgaus made in a slightly off-dry style will do as well. The new style of "unwooded" Chardonnay, which emphasizes fruit rather than oak, offers yet another option. Among reds, lighter, fruit-forward styles such as Zinfandel, Beaujolais or Portuguese Primavera can also work surprisingly well with a dish of Thai-style beef and noodles.

Egg dishes, supposedly the bugbear of food and wine pairings, present no real problem. Let the additional ingredients determine the wine; if it's light spinach and cheese frittata or quiche, go with a white, Pinot Grigio, or a lightly oaked or unoaked Chardonnay. If it's a pipérade fragrant with peppers, onions and garlic, go for a Primavera.

Conventional wisdom used to advise against ordering anything a server recommended as the special of the day, since these were likely to have been created by the chef from ingredients whose impending alternate destination was the dumpster, to avoid a nasty blip in the cost-percentage ledger. Fortunately, the younger genera-tion of chefs who now dominate the industry use the specials of the day in the manner of the greatest European chefs, who create fixed-price menus from the finest and freshest ingredients available. If everyone orders the fresh special, the task of ordering wine is radically simplified.

A restaurant is not a good venue for sampling unfamiliar wines by the bottle (especially at restaurant mark-up), so choose a wine you know, based on what everyone is ordering from the menu. It is worth remembering that the least expensive wines usually bear the highest mark-up. More expensive wines in the middle price range, particularly if the vintages are no longer available in local retail liquor outlets, may be marked up less and actually be bargains at the price. Avoid the high end of the list unless you know the mark-up is marginal. A restaurant that marks up a $150 bottle of wine a full 100 percent to $300 doesn't really want to sell it; it's part of the decor.

B.Y.O.B. (Bring Your Own Bottle) is common in many countries, but rare in North America. However, if you have a special bottle saved for a special occasion (one not available from the restaurant's list), most will allow you to bring it in and charge only a small "corkage" fee for service. It's the individual manager's decision, so always call ahead with your reservation and explain about the wine, making sure they leave a note for the evening staff. If the restaurant agrees, it's only polite to increase the tip accordingly and, especially if the wine is rare, to offer a glass to the manager and the server.

ordering wine at a restaurant

ordering wine at a restaurant

Wines by the Glass

Restaurants used to encourage the sales of heavily marked-up wines by the bottle by offering only "house" red and white wines by the glass, usually mephitic local plonks or industrial-grade bulk corrosives from marginal Rhone or Italian subregions long since paved for parking lots. A health-conscious culture, well educated about wine, and more aggressive laws against drinking and driving, have combined to reduce alcohol consumption in restaurants. As a result, most restaurants now offer both a better standard of "house" wine and an expanded selection of more expensive wines by the glass.

While not always cheaper, this option has several advantages. It allows the curious and adventurous diner to sample unfamiliar wines without buying the bottle. It resolves the dilemma of what wine to order for a larger party with varied tastes; let everyone order their own by the glass. It also eliminates the problem of the over-attentive server who continually hovers and tops up your glass after every sip with the aim of emptying the bottle before your main course arrives, in the hope of selling a second bottle and proportionally increasing the size of the percentage tip. If you order by the bottle, you have to keep one eye constantly peeled for the server's approach, ready to put your hand over your glass without knocking it over while maintaining eye contact and the appearance of attention to your dining companions.

Years of dining in restaurants taught me to let the server go through the formal ritual of opening the bottle and pouring the first glass, then say, politely but firmly, "I know you have other tables to take care of and we don't mind pouring our own wine." Most servers took the hint. If they didn't, I said, "I'm in the business myself and I know how busy you are. I'll handle the wine, you handle the food and we'll split the tip." Weary of game-playing and bills inflated by half-finished bottles, now I simply order a glass at a time.

Ordering wines by the glass allows the diner to both control and precisely monitor consumption. When your glass is constantly topped up from a bottle, you might have consumed two, three or four glasses. You can't always tell, since food absorbs wine and slows its progress into your bloodstream, but the Breathalyzer at the roadblock down the street can. If you order by the glass, you only have to consult the bill to decide if you should have the valet bring the Rolls around or call a cab.

A useful tip: when ordering wines by the glass, stick to the lower end of the list. Despite the best efforts of wine bars and restaurants, most of which use gadgets that remove the air from opened bottles, a wine that sells for $10 a glass probably doesn't move that briskly. The wine may be partially oxidized; at best it will taste somewhat stale. Order wines from the lower or middle price ranges, which enjoy faster turnover.

ordering wine at a restaurant

RESTAURANTS VISITED

restaurants visited

RESTAURANTS VISITED

name

phone   date

hours   companions

menu favorites

wine favorites

memorable chef or staff

comments

○ ✳   ○ ✳✳   ○ ✳✳✳   ○ $ ○ $$ ○ $$$
       pleasure   spending

RESTAURANTS VISITED

name
_____

phone
_____

date
_____

hours
_____

companions
_____

menu favorites
_____

wine favorites
_____

memorable chef or staff
_____

comments
_____

_____

_____

○ ✱   ○ ✱✱   ○ ✱✱✱
pleasure

○ $ ○ $$ ○ $$$
spending

visited

RESTAURANTS VISITED

_____

name

_____

phone

_____

date

_____

hours

_____

companions

_____

menu favorites

_____

wine favorites

_____

memorable chef or staff

_____

comments

_____

_____

_____

○ ✳   ○ ✳✳   ○ ✳✳✳   ○ $ ○ $$ ○ $$$
pleasure   spending

RESTAURANTS VISITED

name

phone‚

date

hours

companions

menu favorites

wine favorites

memorable chef or staff

comments

○ ✳   ○ ✳✳   ○ ✳✳✳
pleasure

○ $ ○ $$ ○ $$$
spending

RESTAURANTS VISITED

name

phone

date

hours

companions

menu favorites

wine favorites

memorable chef or staff

comments

○ ✳   ○ ✳✳   ○ ✳✳✳   ○ $ ○ $ $ ○ $ $ $
pleasure   spending

RESTAURANTS VISITED

name

phone   date

hours   companions

menu favorites

wine favorites

memorable chef or staff

comments

○ ✳   ○ ✳✳   ○ ✳✳✳   ○ $ ○ $$ ○ $$$
pleasure   spending

RESTAURANTS VISITED

name

phone

date

hours

companions

menu favorites

wine favorites

memorable chef or staff

comments

○ ✳   ○ ✳✳   ○ ✳✳✳   ○ $ ○ $$ ○ $$$
          pleasure   spending

RESTAURANTS VISITED

name

phone   date

hours   companions

menu favorites

wine favorites

memorable chef or staff

comments

○ ✳   ○ ✳✳   ○ ✳✳✳   ○ $ ○ $$ ○ $$$
       pleasure   spending

visited

RESTAURANTS VISITED

name

phone

date

hours

companions

menu favorites

wine favorites

memorable chef or staff

comments

○ ✳   ○ ✳✳   ○ ✳✳✳   ○ $ ○ $$ ○ $$$
pleasure   spending

RESTAURANTS VISITED

name

phone   date

hours   companions

menu favorites

wine favorites

memorable chef or staff

comments

○ ✱   ○ ✱✱   ○ ✱✱✱   ○ $ ○ $$ ○ $$$
       pleasure   spending

visited

RESTAURANTS VISITED

name

phone   date

hours   companions

menu favorites

wine favorites

memorable chef or staff

comments

○ **✳**   ○ **✳✳**   ○ **✳✳✳**   ○ **$**   ○ **$$**   ○ **$$$**
         pleasure   spending

RESTAURANTS VISITED

name

phone

date

hours

companions

menu favorites

wine favorites

memorable chef or staff

comments

○ ✳   ○ ✳✳   ○ ✳✳✳
       pleasure

○ $ ○ $$ ○ $$$
       spending

visited

RESTAURANTS VISITED

name

phone   date

hours   companions

menu favorites

wine favorites

memorable chef or staff

comments

○ ✳   ○ ✳✳   ○ ✳✳✳   ○ $ ○ $$ ○ $$$
pleasure   spending

RESTAURANTS VISITED

name

phone

date

hours

companions

menu favorites

wine favorites

memorable chef or staff

comments

○ ✳   ○ ✳✳   ○ ✳✳✳   ○ $ ○ $$ ○ $$$
pleasure   spending

RESTAURANTS VISITED

name

phone

date

hours

companions

menu favorites

wine favorites

memorable chef or staff

comments

○ ✳   ○ ✳✳   ○ ✳✳✳   ○ $ ○ $$ ○ $$$
pleasure   spending

RESTAURANTS VISITED

name

phone   date

hours   companions

menu favorites

wine favorites

memorable chef or staff

comments

⊙ ✶   ⊙ ✶✶   ⊙ ✶✶✶   ⊙ $ ⊙ $$ ⊙ $$$
      pleasure   spending

RESTAURANTS VISITED

name

phone

date

hours

companions

menu favorites

wine favorites

memorable chef or staff

comments

○ ✳   ○ ✳✳   ○ ✳✳✳   ○ $ ○ $$ ○ $$$
pleasure   spending

RESTAURANTS VISITED

name

phone   date

hours   companions

menu favorites

wine favorites

memorable chef or staff

comments

○ *   ○ **   ○ ***   ○ $ ○ $$ ○ $$$
        pleasure   spending

RESTAURANTS VISITED

name
_____

phone
_____

date

hours
_____

companions

menu favorites
_____

wine favorites
_____

memorable chef or staff
_____

comments
_____

_____

_____

○ ✳   ○ ✳✳   ○ ✳✳✳   ○ $ ○ $$ ○ $$$
                    pleasure   spending

RESTAURANTS VISITED

name

phone   date

hours   companions

menu favorites

wine favorites

memorable chef or staff

comments

○ ✳   ○ ✳✳   ○ ✳✳✳   ○ $ ○ $$ ○ $$$
      pleasure   spending

visited

RESTAURANTS VISITED

name

phone   date

hours   companions

menu favorites

wine favorites

memorable chef or staff

comments

○ ✳   ○ ✳✳   ○ ✳✳✳   ○ $ ○ $$ ○ $$$
          pleasure   spending

RESTAURANTS VISITED

name

phone

date

hours

companions

menu favorites

wine favorites

memorable chef or staff

comments

○ ✳   ○ ✳✳   ○ ✳✳✳
pleasure

○ $ ○ $ $ ○ $ $ $
spending

RESTAURANTS VISITED

name

phone

date

hours

companions

menu favorites

wine favorites

memorable chef or staff

comments

○ *   ○ **   ○ ***
pleasure

○ $ ○ $$ ○ $$$
spending

RESTAURANTS VISITED

name

phone   date

hours   companions

menu favorites

wine favorites

memorable chef or staff

comments

○ ✱   ○ ✱✱   ○ ✱✱✱   ○ $ ○ $$ ○ $$$
pleasure   spending

RESTAURANTS VISITED

name

phone

date

hours

companions

menu favorites

wine favorites

memorable chef or staff

comments

○ ✳   ○ ✳✳   ○ ✳✳✳
pleasure

○ $ ○ $$ ○ $$$
spending

RESTAURANTS VISITED

name

phone

date

hours

companions

menu favorites

wine favorites

memorable chef or staff

comments

○ ✳   ○ ✳✳   ○ ✳✳✳
pleasure

○ $ ○ $$ ○ $$$
spending

visited

RESTAURANTS VISITED

name

phone

date

hours

companions

menu favorites

wine favorites

memorable chef or staff

comments

○ ✱   ○ ✱✱   ○ ✱✱✱   ○ $ ○ $$ ○ $$$
pleasure   spending

RESTAURANTS VISITED

name

phone

date

hours

companions

menu favorites

wine favorites

memorable chef or staff

comments

○ ✳ ○ ✳✳ ○ ✳✳✳
pleasure

○ $ ○ $$ ○ $$$
spending

visited

RESTAURANTS VISITED

name

phone

date

hours

companions

menu favorites

wine favorites

memorable chef or staff

comments

○ ✳   ○ ✳✳   ○ ✳✳✳
pleasure

○ $ ○ $ $ ○ $ $ $
spending

name

phone

date

hours

companions

menu favorites

wine favorites

memorable chef or staff

comments

○ ✳   ○ ✳✳   ○ ✳✳✳   ○ $ ○ $$ ○ $$$

pleasure   spending

RESTAURANTS VISITED

name

phone

date

hours

companions

menu favorites

wine favorites

memorable chef or staff

comments

○ ✱   ○ ✱✱   ○ ✱✱✱   ○ $ ○ $$ ○ $$$
pleasure   spending

visited   52

name

phone

date

hours

companions

menu favorites

wine favorites

memorable chef or staff

comments

○ ✳   ○ ✳✳   ○ ✳✳✳
pleasure

○ $ ○ $ $ ○ $ $ $
spending

RESTAURANTS VISITED

name
_____

phone _____ date _____

hours _____ companions _____

menu favorites
_____

wine favorites
_____

memorable chef or staff
_____

comments
_____

_____

_____

○ ✳   ○ ✳✳   ○ ✳✳✳   ○ $ ○ $$ ○ $$$
pleasure   spending

RESTAURANTS VISITED

name

phone   date

hours   companions

menu favorites

wine favorites

memorable chef or staff

comments

○ ✳   ○ ✳✳   ○ ✳✳✳   ○ $ ○ $$ ○ $$$
        pleasure   spending

RESTAURANTS VISITED

name

phone

date

hours

companions

menu favorites

wine favorites

memorable chef or staff

comments

○ ✳   ○ ✳✳   ○ ✳✳✳   ○ $ ○ $$ ○ $$$
        pleasure   spending

RESTAURANTS VISITED

name
_____

phone _____   date _____

hours _____   companions _____

menu favorites
_____

wine favorites
_____

memorable chef or staff
_____

comments
_____

_____

_____

○ ✳   ○ ✳✳   ○ ✳✳✳   ○ $ ○ $$ ○ $$$
       pleasure   spending

RESTAURANTS VISITED

name

phone   date

hours   companions

menu favorites

wine favorites

memorable chef or staff

comments

    ○ ✳   ○ ✳✳   ○ ✳✳✳   ○ $ ○ $$ ○ $$$
            pleasure   spending

RESTAURANTS VISITED

name

phone

date

hours

companions

menu favorites

wine favorites

memorable chef or staff

comments

○ ✳   ○ ✳✳   ○ ✳✳✳   ○ $ ○ $$ ○ $$$
pleasure   spending

visited

RESTAURANTS VISITED

name

phone

date

hours

companions

menu favorites

wine favorites

memorable chef or staff

comments

○ ✷   ○ ✷✷   ○ ✷✷✷   ○ $ ○ $$ ○ $$$
        pleasure   spending

name

phone

date

hours

companions

menu favorites

wine favorites

memorable chef or staff

comments

○ ✳   ○ ✳✳   ○ ✳✳✳
pleasure

○ $ ○ $$ ○ $$$
spending

RESTAURANTS VISITED

name

phone   date

hours   companions

menu favorites

wine favorites

memorable chef or staff

comments

○ ✳   ○ ✳✳   ○ ✳✳✳   ○ $ ○ $$ ○ $$$
       pleasure   spending

RESTAURANTS VISITED

name

phone   date

hours   companions

menu favorites

wine favorites

memorable chef or staff

comments

○ ✳   ○ ✳✳   ○ ✳✳✳   ○ $ ○ $$ ○ $$$
            pleasure   spending

RESTAURANTS VISITED

name

phone   date

hours   companions

menu favorites

wine favorites

memorable chef or staff

comments

○ ✳   ○ ✳✳   ○ ✳✳✳   ○ $ ○ $$ ○ $$$
       pleasure   spending

RESTAURANTS VISITED

name

phone   date

hours   companions

menu favorites

wine favorites

memorable chef or staff

comments

○ ✻   ○ ✻✻   ○ ✻✻✻   ○ $ ○ $$ ○ $$$
         pleasure   spending

RESTAURANTS VISITED

name

phone   date

hours   companions

menu favorites

wine favorites

memorable chef or staff

comments

○ ✳   ○ ✳✳   ○ ✳✳✳   ○ $ ○ $$ ○ $$$
        pleasure   spending

RESTAURANTS VISITED

name

phone

date

hours

companions

menu favorites

wine favorites

memorable chef or staff

comments

○ ✳   ○ ✳✳   ○ ✳✳✳
pleasure

○ $ ○ $$ ○ $$$
spending

RESTAURANTS VISITED

name

phone

date

hours

companions

menu favorites

wine favorites

memorable chef or staff

comments

○ ✳   ○ ✳✳   ○ ✳✳✳   ○ $ ○ $$ ○ $$$
pleasure   spending

name

phone

date

hours

companions

menu favorites

wine favorites

memorable chef or staff

comments

○ ✳   ○ ✳✳   ○ ✳✳✳
pleasure

○ $ ○ $$ ○ $$$
spending

RESTAURANTS TO VISIT

restaurants to visit

RESTAURANTS TO VISIT

name

address

phone

hours

style of dining

recommended by

dishes to try

paste write-ups here

RESTAURANTS TO VISIT

name

address

phone   hours

style of dining   recommended by

dishes to try

paste write-ups here

RESTAURANTS TO VISIT

name

address

phone   hours

style of dining   recommended by

dishes to try

paste write-ups here

RESTAURANTS TO VISIT

name

address

phone   hours

style of dining   recommended by

dishes to try

paste write-ups here

75

to visit

RESTAURANTS TO VISIT

name

address

phone

hours

style of dining

recommended by

dishes to try

paste write-ups here

RESTAURANTS TO VISIT

name

address

phone   hours

style of dining   recommended by

dishes to try

paste write-ups here

RESTAURANTS TO VISIT

name

address

phone

hours

style of dining

recommended by

dishes to try

paste write-ups here

RESTAURANTS TO VISIT

name

address

phone   hours

style of dining   recommended by

dishes to try

paste write-ups here

RESTAURANTS TO VISIT

_____
name

_____
address

_____   _____
phone   hours

_____   _____
style of dining   recommended by

_____
dishes to try

paste write-ups here

RESTAURANTS TO VISIT

name

address

phone

hours

style of dining

recommended by

dishes to try

paste write-ups here

restaurants to visit

RESTAURANTS TO VISIT

name
_____

address
_____

phone _____   hours _____

style of dining _____   recommended by _____

dishes to try
_____

paste write-ups here

RESTAURANTS TO VISIT

name

address

phone   hours

style of dining   recommended by

dishes to try

paste write-ups here

RESTAURANTS TO VISIT

name
_____

address
_____

phone _____   hours _____

style of dining _____   recommended by _____

dishes to try
_____

paste write-ups here

RESTAURANTS TO VISIT

name

address

phone   hours

style of dining   recommended by

dishes to try

paste write-ups here

RESTAURANTS TO VISIT

name

address

phone

hours

style of dining

recommended by

dishes to try

paste write-ups here

RESTAURANTS TO VISIT

name

address

phone   hours

style of dining   recommended by

dishes to try

paste write-ups here

RESTAURANTS TO VISIT

restaurants to visit

name

address

phone

hours

style of dining

recommended by

dishes to try

paste write-ups here

RESTAURANTS TO VISIT

name

address

phone

hours

style of dining

recommended by

dishes to try

paste write-ups here

RESTAURANTS TO VISIT

name

address

phone   hours

style of dining   recommended by

dishes to try

paste write-ups here

RESTAURANTS TO VISIT

name

address

phone   hours

style of dining   recommended by

dishes to try

paste write-ups here

RESTAURANTS TO VISIT

name

address

phone

hours

style of dining

recommended by

dishes to try

paste write-ups here

RESTAURANTS TO VISIT

name

address

phone

hours

style of dining

recommended by

dishes to try

paste write-ups here

RESTAURANTS TO VISIT

name
_____

address
_____

phone   hours
_____

style of dining   recommended by
_____

dishes to try
_____

paste write-ups here

RESTAURANTS TO VISIT

_____
name

_____
address

_____   _____
phone   hours

_____   _____
style of dining   recommended by

_____
dishes to try

paste write-ups here

RESTAURANTS TO VISIT

name

address

phone

hours

style of dining

recommended by

dishes to try

paste write-ups here

RESTAURANTS TO VISIT

name

address

phone

hours

style of dining

recommended by

dishes to try

paste write-ups here

RESTAURANTS TO VISIT

name

address

phone

hours

style of dining

recommended by

dishes to try

paste write-ups here

RESTAURANTS TO VISIT

name

address

phone

hours

style of dining

recommended by

dishes to try

paste write-ups here

RESTAURANT REVIEWS

restaurant reviews

RESTAURANT REVIEWS

paste write-up here

reviews

paste business card here

RESTAURANT REVIEWS

paste write-up here

paste business card here

RESTAURANT REVIEWS

reviews

paste write-up here

paste business card here

RESTAURANT REVIEWS

paste write-up here

reviews

paste business card here

RESTAURANT REVIEWS

reviews

paste write-up here

paste business card here

RESTAURANT REVIEWS

paste write-up here

reviews

paste business card here

RESTAURANT REVIEWS

reviews

paste write-up here

paste business card here

RESTAURANT REVIEWS

paste write-up here

paste business card here

RESTAURANT REVIEWS

paste write-up here

paste business card here

RESTAURANT REVIEWS

paste write-up here

paste business card here

RESTAURANT REVIEWS

reviews

paste write-up here

paste business card here

RESTAURANT REVIEWS

paste write-up here

paste business card here

RESTAURANT REVIEWS

reviews

paste write-up here

paste business card here

paste write-up here

reviews

paste business card here

RESTAURANT REVIEWS

reviews

paste write-up here

paste business card here

RESTAURANT REVIEWS

paste write-up here

reviews

paste business card here

RESTAURANT REVIEWS

reviews

paste write-up here

paste business card here

RESTAURANT REVIEWS

paste write-up here

paste business card here

RESTAURANT REVIEWS

reviews

paste write-up here

paste business card here

RESTAURANT REVIEWS

paste write-up here

paste business card here

RESTAURANT REVIEWS

paste write-up here

paste business card here

paste write-up here

reviews

paste business card here

RESTAURANT REVIEWS

reviews

paste write-up here

paste business card here

RESTAURANT REVIEWS

paste write-up here

paste business card here

GRATUITY CHART

$ Amount	10%	15%	20%
10	1.00	1.50	2.00
20	2.00	3.00	4.00
30	3.00	4.50	6.00
40	4.00	6.00	8.00
50	5.00	7.50	10.00
60	6.00	9.00	12.00
70	7.00	10.50	14.00
80	8.00	12.00	16.00
90	9.00	13.50	18.00
100	10.00	15.00	20.00
110	11.00	16.50	22.00
120	12.00	18.00	24.00
130	13.00	19.50	26.00
140	14.00	21.00	28.00
150	15.00	22.50	30.00
160	16.00	24.00	32.00
170	17.00	25.50	34.00
180	18.00	27.00	36.00
190	19.00	28.50	38.00
200	20.00	30.00	40.00
210	21.00	31.50	42.00
220	22.00	33.00	44.00
230	23.00	34.50	46.00
240	24.00	36.00	48.00
250	25.00	37.50	50.00
260	26.00	39.00	52.00
270	27.00	40.50	54.00
280	28.00	42.00	56.00
290	29.00	43.50	58.00
300	30.00	45.00	60.00

Customary tipping in Canada is 10-15% of the total bill (without taxes).
Customary tipping in the U.S. is 15-20% of the total bill (without taxes).